INDIANA
Macmillan/McGraw-Hill TIMELINKS

People and Places

PROGRAM AUTHORS

James A. Banks
Kevin P. Colleary
Linda Greenow
Walter C. Parker
Emily M. Schell
Dinah Zike

CONTRIBUTORS

Raymond C. Jones
Irma M. Olmedo

Macmillan/McGraw-Hill

Economics

PROGRAM AUTHORS

James A. Banks, Ph.D.
Kerry and Linda Killinger Professor
of Diversity Studies and Director, Center
for Multicultural Education
University of Washington
Seattle, Washington

Kevin P. Colleary, Ed.D.
Curriculum and Teaching Department
Graduate School of Education
Fordham University
New York, New York

Linda Greenow, Ph.D.
Associate Professor and Chair
Department of Geography
State University of New York at New Paltz
New Paltz, New York

Walter C. Parker, Ph.D.
Professor of Social Studies Education,
Adjunct Professor of Political Science
University of Washington
Seattle, Washington

Emily M. Schell, Ed.D.
Visiting Professor, Teacher Education
San Diego State University
San Diego, California

Dinah Zike
Educational Consultant
Dinah-Mite Activities, Inc.
San Antonio, Texas

CONTRIBUTORS

Raymond C. Jones, Ph.D.
Director of Secondary Social Studies
Education
Wake Forest University
Winston-Salem, North Carolina

Irma M. Olmedo
Associate Professor
University of Illinois-Chicago
College of Education
Chicago, Illinois

HISTORIANS/SCHOLARS

Larry Dale, Ph.D.
Director, Center for Economic Education
Arkansas State University
Jonesboro, Arkansas

GRADE LEVEL REVIEWERS

Brigid Kemper
Second Grade Teacher
Brook Park Elementary School
Indianapolis, Indiana

Kathleen Clark
Second Grade Teacher
Edison Elementary School
Fraser, Michigan

Patricia Hinchliff
Second Grade Teacher
West Woods School
Hamden, Connecticut

Pamela South
Second Grade Teacher
Greenwood Elementary School
Princess Anne, Maryland

Karen Starr
Second Grade Teacher
Arthur Froberg Elementary School
Rockford, Illinois

EDITORIAL ADVISORY BOARD

Bradley R. Bakle
Assistant Superintendent
East Allen County Schools
New Haven, Indiana

Marilyn Barr
Assistant Superintendent for Instruction
Clyde-Savannah Central School
Clyde, New York

Lisa Bogle
Elementary Coordinator, K-5
Rutherford County Schools
Murfreesboro, Tennessee

Janice Buselt
Campus Support, Primary and ESOL
Wichita Public Schools
Wichita, Kansas

Kathy Cassioppi
Social Studies Coordinator
Rockford Public Schools, District 205
Rockford, Illinois

Denise Johnson, Ph.D.
Social Studies Supervisor
Knox County Schools
Knoxville, Tennessee

Steven Klein, Ph.D.
Social Studies Coordinator
Illinois School District U-46
Elgin, Illinois

Sondra Markman
Curriculum Director
Warren Township Board of Education
Warren Township, New Jersey

Cathy Nelson
Social Studies Coordinator
Columbus Public Schools
Columbus, Ohio

Holly Pies
Social Studies Coordinator
Vigo County Schools
Terre Haute, Indiana

Avon Ruffin
Social Studies County Supervisor
Winston-Salem/Forsyth Schools
Lewisville, North Carolina

Chuck Schierloh
Social Studies Curriculum Team Leader
Lima City Schools
Lima, Ohio

Bob Shamy
Social Studies Supervisor
East Brunswick Public Schools
East Brunswick, New Jersey

Judy Trujillo
Social Studies Coordinator
Columbia Missouri School District
Columbia, Missouri

Todd Wigginton
Coordinator of Social Studies K-12
Metropolitan Nashville Public Schools
Nashville, Tennessee

The McGraw-Hill Companies

Macmillan McGraw-Hill

Copyright © 2010 by The McGraw-Hill Companies, Inc. All rights reserved. Except as permitted under the United States Copyright Act, no part of this publication may be reproduced or distributed in any form or by any means, or stored in a database or retrieval system, without prior permission of the publisher.
Send all inquires to: Macmillan/McGraw-Hill, 8787 Orion Place, Columbus, OH 43240-4027

MHID 0-02-153377-6   ISBN 978-0-02-153377-0   Printed in the United States of America

3 4 5 6 7 8 9 10   058/043   13 12 11 10 09

People and Places
Table of Contents

Unit 4 Needs and Wants

 How do we get the things we need and want? 1

People, Places, and Events 2

Lesson 1 Our Needs and Wants 4
  Place Savings Bank 9

Lesson 2 Many Kinds of Work 12
  People George Washington Carver 15
  Event Walking to Help Others 16
  Chart and Graph Skills Bar Graph 18

Lesson 3 Goods and Trade 20
  Around the World Chile 21
Citizenship **Democracy in Action**
  Cooperating 26

Lesson 4 Producers and Consumers 28
  Chart and Graph Skills Flow Chart 30
Map and Globe Skills Follow Routes on a Map 34

Review and Assess 36

Glossary R1

Index R4

Credits/Acknowledgments R6

Skills and Features

Map and Globe Skills
Follow Routes on a Map   34

Chart and Graph Skills
Bar Graph   18
Flow Chart   30

People, Places, and Events
Place Savings Bank   9
People George Washington Carver   15
Event Walking to Help Others   16

Around the World   Chile   21

Citizenship   Democracy in Action
Cooperating   26

Maps

The United States Trades with Nigeria   24
Truck Route   34
School Bus Route   37

Needs and Wants

EXPLORE
The
Big
Idea

How do we get the things we need and want?

LOG ON Find out more about needs and wants at www.macmillanmh.com

LEMONA 25¢

People, Places, and Events

A Corn Farmer

This **farmer** grows corn.

A Farm in Indiana

Corn is grown on this **farm** in Indiana.

Selling Corn

Farmers **sell their corn** at this farmers' market.

3

Vocabulary

needs

shelter

wants

scarce

save

technology

Reading Skill

Sequence

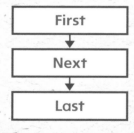

First

↓

Next

↓

Last

Our Needs and Wants

What Are Needs and Wants?

Needs are things that people must have to live. Families need food, clothing, love, and **shelter**. A shelter is a place to live.

People also have **wants**. Wants are things people like to have but do not need. Toys and games are wants. We like to have them, but we do not need them to live.

 Which pictures show needs? Wants?

Needs	Wants

How Do We Choose?

The Park family has food, clothing, and other things they need to live. They still have money left to buy things they want. What does the Park family want?

They want to buy a computer. They also want to go on a family trip. But they do not have enough money for both. They have to choose.

or

They choose to buy a computer. They have to give up buying the family trip. The thing people give up to buy something else is called the *opportunity cost*. The family trip is the Park family's opportunity cost.

 What is opportunity cost?

Ana does not have enough money.

Ana saves her money.

Saving Money

Ana wants to buy an MP3 player. But she does not have enough money. When there is not enough of something, it is called **scarce**. Money is scarce for Ana.

There is something you can do when money is scarce. You can **save** your money. Save means to keep your money to use later.

Ana rakes leaves for her neighbors to earn money. To earn means to be paid for work you do.

Each time Ana earns money, she saves some. Soon, she will have enough money to buy the MP3 player.

 What can you do when money is scarce?

Ana buys an MP3 player.

Places
Savings Bank

A bank is a place where people can save money. A bank keeps the money safe.

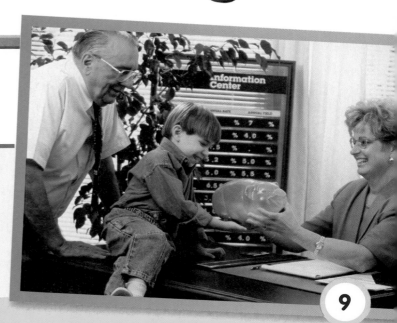

New Technology

New **technology** has changed the way we live. Technology is the science of making things faster, easier, or better.

Years ago, computers were very large. One computer took up a whole room! Today, computers are everywhere. They are in our homes, schools, and work places.

Long ago, people did not have MP3 players or DVDs. Today, we have e-mail, cell phones, and robots. New technology has made our lives easier and more fun.

 How does technology help us?

Check Understanding

1. **Vocabulary** Why is **shelter** a need and not a want?

2. **Sequence** What steps did Ana follow to buy an MP3 player?

First
↓
Next
↓
Last

3. Why do people sometimes need to make choices?

Vocabulary

service

tax

volunteer

bar graph

Reading Skill

Sequence

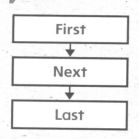

First
↓
Next
↓
Last

Many Kinds Of Work

Working to Earn Money

Most people work to earn money to buy the things they need and want. A barber cuts hair. A florist works with flowers. A scientist works to understand and explain nature. What kind of work would you like to do?

What are some other jobs people do to earn money?

florist

scientist

Services

Some people have **service** jobs. A service is something useful that people do for others. A doctor helps people who are sick. A teacher helps us learn. These are both service jobs.

art teacher

doctor

Some people have service jobs that are paid for by the community. The money used to pay them is called **tax**.

Tax money is used to pay mail carriers, police officers, and firefighters. Can you think of other service workers in your community?

mail carrier

 What does some tax money pay for?

People
George Washington Carver

George Washington Carver was a teacher. He taught people about farming. He said, "Education is the key to unlock the golden door of freedom."

Volunteer Workers

Not all workers earn money. Some workers are **volunteers**. A volunteer is a person who works for no pay to help others. Volunteers help because they care.

Some volunteers visit older people who are alone. This volunteer is helping the woman take her medicine.

Event
Walking to Help Others

These volunteers help people who are sick. They walk for miles. People pay money for every mile that the volunteers walk. The money is given to help sick people.

These volunteers work for *Habitat for Humanity*. They help build houses for people who have none.

 What are some ways to volunteer?

Children Volunteers

Children can be volunteers, too. Ms. Rose's class collected winter clothes for people who do not have money to buy them.

They made a **bar graph** that shows how many clothes they collected. A bar graph uses bars to show and compare information. How many hats were collected?

Winter Clothes Collected

Children can collect money to help people, too. These children had a craft and bake sale. The money was used to help people who have cancer.

 How can children volunteer?

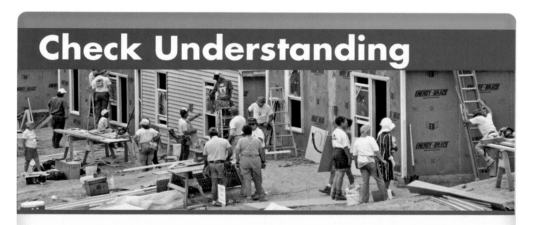

Check Understanding

1. **Vocabulary** What is a **volunteer**?

2. **Sequence** How can walking help people who are sick?

First
Next
Last

3. EXPLORE The Big Idea How does work help people get the things they need and want?

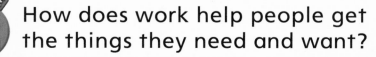

Goods and Trade

Lesson 3

Vocabulary

goods

factory

trade

Reading Skill

Sequence

First
↓
Next
↓
Last

Growing Goods

Things grown or made to sell are called **goods**. Flowers are goods that farmers grow to sell. Corn, pumpkins, and apples are goods grown by farmers, too.

Goods grown on farms can be sold at stores and markets. We shop at stores and markets to buy the goods we need and want.

 Can you name other goods that farmers grow?

Around the World

Chile is a country in South America. Many farmers in Chile grow goods. They sell their goods at stores and markets just like we do in the United States.

Making Goods

Some goods are made. Clothes, books, and toys are all goods that are made for people to sell and buy.

Ann is making a good to sell! She is making lemonade. Ann will sell the lemonade at a stand outside her home.

Many goods are made in a building called a **factory**. Clothes, books, and toys are made in factories. Cheese can be made in a factory, too.

In a cheese factory, cheese is made from milk. Workers use machines to make, cut, and wrap the cheese to sell.

 What are two kinds of goods?

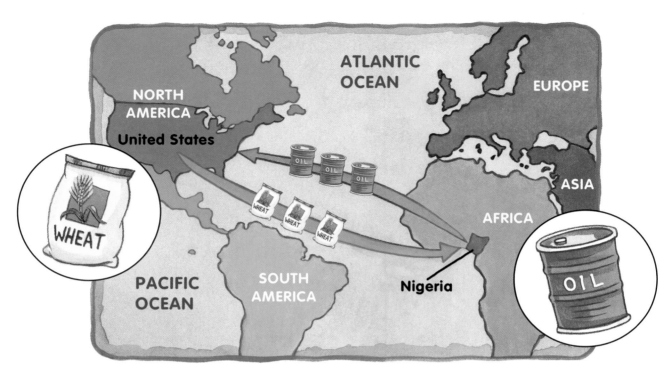

Countries Trade

Many countries make or grow more goods than they need. They can **trade** these goods with other countries. Trade means to give something and then get something back.

The United States grows a lot of wheat. The country of Nigeria has a lot of oil. The United States trades with Nigeria.

When countries trade, they pay money to buy the goods they need or want. The United States pays money to Nigeria for oil. Nigeria pays money to the United States for wheat.

 What is trade?

Check Understanding

1. **Vocabulary** What is a **factory**?

2. **Sequence** How does the United States trade with Nigeria?

First
Next
Last

3. How do we get the goods we need or want?

Citizenship

Democracy in Action

Cooperating

People cooperate by working together. Cooperating helps people get along and get things done. Read what happened when Juan told Clay why he could not play ball.

Clay helped Juan by cooperating.
What would you do?

Hey, Juan!
Can you
go with me to
play ball?

No, I have to finish
raking these leaves.

We can cooperate.
You rake and I will
bag. Then, we can
play ball!

Lesson 4

Vocabulary
producer

consumer

Reading Skill
Sequence

First
↓
Next
↓
Last

Producers and Consumers

Producers

In Lesson 3 you learned that goods are things people make or grow to sell. The people who make or grow the goods are called **producers**.

The producer you see on page 28 makes violins to sell. The potato farmers below are producers, too. They grow potatoes to sell.

 What does a producer do?

1. Producers, like this farmer, grow the apples.

2. Truck drivers take the apples to stores.

From Farm to You

Many people work together to bring us the goods we buy and use. The flow chart shows how we get apples, starting with the producer and ending with the **consumer**.

A consumer is a person who buys or uses goods. He or she buys and uses the goods grown or made by producers.

 What happens last in the chart?

3. Store workers sell the apples.

4. Consumers buy the apples.

We Are All Consumers

Everyone is a consumer. That is because we all have needs and wants. When a farmer grows apples to sell, the farmer is a producer. If the same farmer buys an apple pie from a baker, the farmer is a consumer.

Rachel and her mom are both consumers. Rachel's mom bought her this violin. But Rachel is the one who is using it!

 How are you a consumer?

Check Understanding

1. **Vocabulary** What is a **consumer**?

2. **Sequence** How do apples go from a farm to a store?

First
Next
Last

3. How is a farmer both a consumer and a producer?

Vocabulary

route

Follow Routes on a Map

A **route** is a way of going from one place to another. You can follow a route on a map. Red arrows show the route.

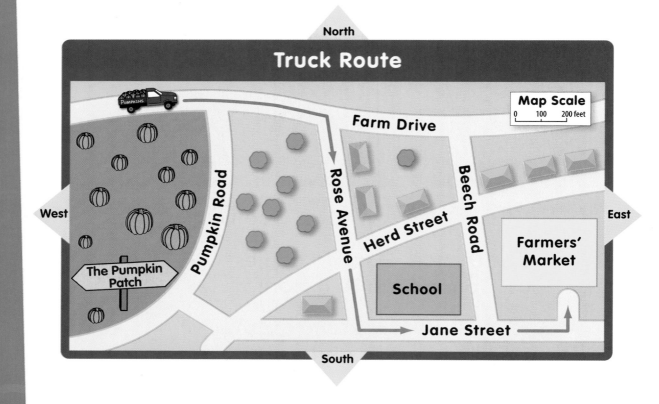

North

Truck Route

Farm Drive

Map Scale
0   100   200 feet

West

Pumpkin Road

Rose Avenue

Herd Street

Beech Road

East

The Pumpkin Patch

Farmers' Market

School

Jane Street

South

Look at the Truck Route map on page 34. Find the Pumpkin Patch truck on Farm Drive. Next, find the Farmers' Market.

The driver is bringing pumpkins to the Farmers' Market to sell. Follow the arrows from the Pumpkin Patch truck to the Farmers' Market.

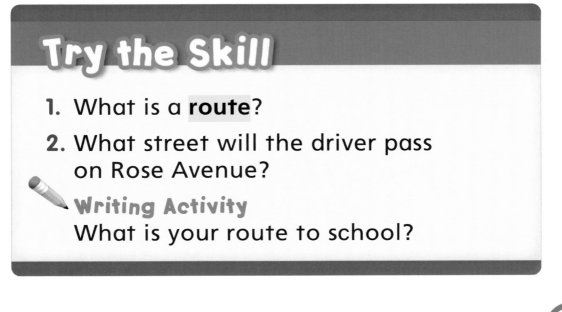

Try the Skill

1. What is a **route**?
2. What street will the driver pass on Rose Avenue?

✎ **Writing Activity**
What is your route to school?

Vocabulary

Choose the vocabulary word that best completes each sentence.

tax   **save**   **service**

1. A _____ is something useful that people do for others.

2. People pay _____ money to help their communities.

3. You can _____ money to use later.

Critical Thinking

4. In a store, what do you trade for the goods you buy?

5. Why can we not buy everything we want?

Skill

Follow Routes on a Map

Look at the map. Then answer the question.

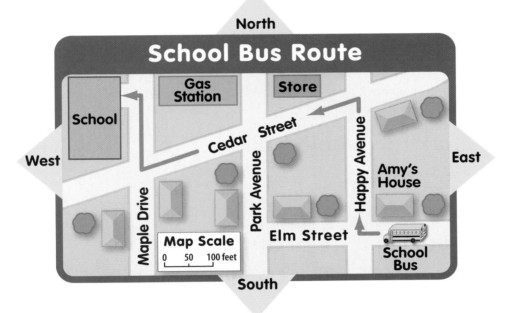

6. On what street does the bus drive past a store and a gas station?

   A. Maple Drive

   B. Elm Street

   C. Park Avenue

   D. Cedar Street

Economics Activity

Make a Job Cartoon

1 Write "Goods" and "Services" on a sheet of paper.

2 Cut out pictures of working people from magazines.

3 Glue a picture of a producer on the "Goods" side, and a service worker on the "Services" side.

4 Write a speech bubble for each worker.

Picture Glossary

bar graph A graph that uses bars to show and compare information. *This **bar graph** shows how many of each kind of clothing Ms. Rose's class collected.* (page 18)

consumer Someone who uses the goods made by a producer. *This **consumer** is buying apples.* (page 30)

factory A building where things are made. *Cheese is made in this **factory**.* (page 23)

goods Things that are grown or made to sell. *Flowers are **goods** that are grown on farms and sold at markets.* (page 21)

needs Things that people must have to live. *Food, clothing, love, and shelter are **needs**.* (page 5)

producer A worker who grows or makes goods to sell. *These farmers are **producers** who grow potatoes.* (page 29)

route A way of going from one place to another. *He took the shortest route to drive from the Pumpkin Patch to the Farmers' Market.* (page 34)

save To keep money to use later. *I can save my money to buy something I want.* (page 8)

scarce When there is not enough of something. *Ana wants to buy an MP3 player, but her money is scarce.* (page 8)

service Something useful that people do for others. *This doctor does a service by helping Sarah get better.* (page 14)

shelter A place where people live. *We need shelter to protect us from the weather.* (page 5)

tax Money that people pay to a community. *Schools are built with tax money from the community.* (page 15)

technology The science of making things faster, easier, or better. *New computer technology has made it easier to find information.* (page 10)

trade To give something and then get something back. *The United States trades with Nigeria.* (page 24)

V

volunteer A person who works for no pay to help others. *These volunteers help to build homes for people who have none.* (page 16)

W

wants Things people like to have but do not need to live. *Toys and games are wants.* (page 5)

Index

This index lists many things you can find in your book. It tells the page numbers on which they are found. If you see the letter *m* before a page number, you will find a map on that page.

A

Agriculture. *See also* Farmers

B

Banks, 9
Barbers, 13
Bar graphs, 18

C

Carver, George Washington, 15
Cheese, 23
Children as volunteers, 18–19
Chile, 21
Choices, making, 6–7
Citizenship
  Democracy in Action, 26–27
Clothing, 5, 18
Communities and services, 15
Computers, 10
Consumers. *See also* Producers and consumers
Cooperation, 26–27
Corn, 2–3
Countries, 24–25

D

Democracy in Action, 26–27
Doctors, 14

E

Education, 15

F

Factories, 23
Farmers
  as consumers, 32
  as producers, 2–3, 21, 29, 30–31, 32
Firefighters, 15
Florists, 13
Flow charts, 30–31
Flowers, 21
Food, 2, 5, 21
Freedom, 15

G

Games, 5
Goods and trade, 20–25
  See also Producers and consumers
  of countries, 24–25
  job cartoon activity, 38
  making goods, 22–23, 29
  and producers, 29
  trade routes, *m24*

H

Habitat for Humanity, 17
Helping, 16–17
Home, 5, 17

I

Indiana, 2

L

Lemonade stands, 1, 22
Love, 5

M

Machines, 23
Mail carriers, 15
Map and Globe Skills, *m34–35, m37*
Markets, 21, 31
Money
  and banks, 9
  saving, 8–9
  and work, 9, 13

N

Needs and wants, 4–11
  and consumers, 32
  making choices, 6–7
  and opportunity costs, 7
  and saving money, 8–9
  shopping for, 21
  and technology, 10–11
Nigeria, 24–25, *m24*

O

Oil, 24, 25
Opportunity costs, 7

P

People, Places, and Events, 2–3
Police officers, 15
Producers and consumers, 28–33

See also Goods and trade
about, 29
consumers, 30–33
flow chart of, 30–31
producers, 29, 30, 32

Routes, *m34–35, m37*

Saving money, 8–9
Scarcity, 8
Scientists, 13

Senior citizens, caring for, 16
Services, 14–15, 38
Shelter, 5
Sick people, caring for, 16, 19
South America, 21
Stores, 21, 31

Taxes, 15
Teachers, 14, 15
Technology, 10–11
Toys, 5
Trade, 24–25. *See also*
    Goods and trade

United States, 24–25, *m24*

Volunteers, 16–17, 18–19

Credits

Maps XNR

Illustrations
5 Anette Heiberg; 8 Holli Conger; 18 Anette Heiberg; 21 Holli Conger; 23 Eldon Doty; 24 Linda Howard Bittner; 27 Maxie Chambliss 29 Carol Schwartz; 32 Nancy Cote.

Photography Credits All Photographs are by Macmillan/McGraw-hill (MMH) except as noted below.

COV (bl) Bettmann/CORBIS, (br) Pixland/CORBIS, (t) Image Source/SuperStock; i Pixland/CORBIS; 1 Steve Chenn/CORBIS; 2 (bl) Dorling Kindersley/Getty Images, (br) Ike Geib/Grant Heilman Photography, (cl) Scott Sinklier/AgStockUSA; 3 (br) Scott Lanza/Jupiterimages, (c) Larry LeFever/Grant Heilman Photography, (cr) C Squared Studios/Getty Images; 4 Jose Luis Pelaez, Inc./CORBIS; 7 (cl) Ryan McVay/Getty Images, (tr) Charles O; Cecil/Alamy Images; 8 Ken Karp for MMH; 9 (br) David Woods/CORBIS, (tr) Ken Karp for MMH; 10 (b) Ewing Galloway/Index Stock Imagery, (br) er Productions/Getty Images; 11 (c) Charles O; Cecil/Alamy Images, (tr) PunchStock; 12 Adam Crowley/Getty Images; 13 (bl) David Young-Wolff/Getty Images, (br) Mark Harmel/Getty Images; 14 (bl) Jose Luis Pelaez, Inc/PunchStock, (cr) Jose Luis Pelaez, Inc;/CORBIS; 15 (br) Getty Images, (tr) Jeff Dunn/Index Stock Imagery; 16 (br) Kathy McLaughlin/The Image Works, Inc., (cr) Keith Brofsky/Getty Images; 17 (cr) Jeff Greenberg/PhotoEdit, (tc) R; Crandall/The Image Works, Inc; 19 (c) R; Crandall/The Image Works, Inc., (tr) Dan Honda/Contra Costa Times/Zuma Press; 20 John McAnulty/CORBIS; 21 Yadid Levy/Alamy Images; 22 Felicia Martinez/PhotoEdit; 25 (c) John McAnulty/CORBIS, (tr) Photodisc/PunchStock; 26-27 (b) CORBIS; 27 (bl) Ken Karp for MMH; 28 Benjamin F. Fink Jr./Brand X Pictures/PunchStock; 29 Gary Holscher/CORBIS; 30 (tl) Gary Holscher/CORBIS; 30-31 (t) Walter Hodges/CORBIS; 31 (b) Jon Gray/Getty Images, (tr) Tony Freeman/PhotoEdit; 32 Brand X Pictures/PunchStock; 33 (c) Walter Hodges/CORBIS, (tr) Image Source/PunchStock; 35 Cephas Picture Library/Alamy Images; 36 Squared Studios/Getty Images; 38 (br) SW Productions/Getty Images, (cr) CORBIS, (tr) Brand X Pictures/PunchStock; R1 (br) Gary Holscher/CORBIS, (tr) Jon Gray /Getty Images; R2 (br) Photodisc/PunchStock, (cr) Ken Karp for MMH, (cr) Jose Luis Pelaez, Inc/PunchStock, (tr) Ken Karp for MMH; R3 (cr) R; Crandall/The Image Works, Inc.; (tr) Jose Luis Pelaez, Inc;/CORBIS; BKCOV Image Source/SuperStock.